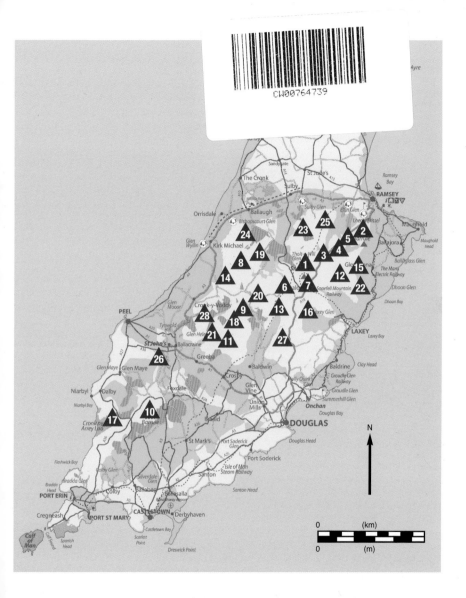

CW00764739

CONTENTS

INTRODUCTION

An undiscovered gem in the British Isles

The Isle of Man is ideal for those who want to walk the hills and achieve every summit of note.

The hilltops are never a great distance from where you can park a car: furthermore the roads often climb high saving the walker much of the hard work! Even the great hill walker Wainwright remarked that few people prefer to walk all the way to their objective if they can be carried there – at least in part – by wheels. The views are always remarkable – both of the Island and across the sea to neighbouring countries. Each trail to the summit reveals hidden secrets often not visible at the start of the journey – little dry valleys, gushing streams, secluded tarns and birds, mammals and flowers that hide until you are almost on top of them.

With only a couple of exceptions, the ascents are easy or moderate rather than tough. And unless you are climbing Snaefell or North Barrule at the weekend you are invariably on your own. Approximately 40% of the Island is unoccupied upland: this provides 80 square miles of hill walking for a population of 80,000 which is swelled by a few thousand walkers visiting from UK. Just across the Irish Sea the Lake District, at 885 square miles, does offer a larger walking terrain but annually over 14 million visitors squeeze into it!

The Island does have three officially designated long distance footpaths which are popular. The Coastal Footpath (Raad ny Foillan) around the entire coastline, the Herring Way (Bayr ny Skeddan) from Peel to Castletown and the Millennium Way which stretches the length of the Island. However, only the Millennium Way has part of its route through the uplands where it tends to favour lower lying terrain and skirts the summits themselves. Thus, the reward for those that make their own way through the hills is invariably solitude: there was only one summit on which I encountered other walkers when researching this guide.

Pure bliss

The hills provide a complete escape from one's everyday life – that is unless you are a farmer who tends his sheep in the uplands! They are places to let go of the busy lives that we lead. I can think of many reasons why I personally cherish my time walking in the hills of the Isle of Man

- Tranquillity. The peacefulness of walking in the hills is the most complete contrast to the noise and bustle of the office, factory, shop, school or wherever you are mainly. Surprisingly, mobile phone reception can be good in the uplands, so switch to 'vibrate only' if you want to minimise disturbance.

- Contemplation. Occasionally you will halt to check the map, but most of the time one's mind wanders off and riffs – untroubled by day-to-day concerns. It is no wonder that one of the most famous poems was conceived when Wordsworth was walking in the Lake District.
- Panorama. The unique and uplifting pleasure of the views from each summit.
- Achievement. The sense of reaching the top, of not being able to go further.
- Adventure. Navigating across country with just map and intuition. Here on the uplands of the Isle of Man are all the ingredients for splendid days of mild adventure.
- Exercise. Regular walking can keep one in shape, and even an occasional walk helps to off-set the pint of beer at the end of the day.
- Educational. Looking at landscapes and terrains awakens an interest in geography – *"How did the land come to look like that?"*
- Companionship: you will always exchange a few words if you pass another walker, it would be absurd not to
- Inexpensive. No Government would ever dare to charge admission!

A gentle challenge

The original idea for the catalogue of hilltops came from my looking at an old map that I was given when I first moved to the Island. The 1:25,000 scale map was published by the Isle of Man Government in 1983 using the imperial measures of feet, yards and miles. I used this, in conjunction with a contemporary OS Landranger Map (sheet 95), to locate 30 points on the uplands marked with a spot height of at least 1,000 feet (305 metres). I have ignored any spot height of this elevation that is marked on a road.

A few of the hilltops are directly accessed by footpaths that are marked clearly on maps and by signposts on the terrain itself. In all cases, footpaths or green lanes will lead you from where you can park a car safely off the road a great proportion of the way. Then with a combination of map, compass and this guide one can cross the remaining terrain to achieve one's goal. The Isle of Man is more enlightened than many parts of the British Isles in that large areas of upland are known as 'public ramblage' which essentially means that one is at liberty to roam at will provided one takes care not to cause damage. Other areas are owned by the Forestry Division and access is not a problem. However, two of the summits are on private land where the owner declares that there is no public access.

The most northerly, and easterly, of the 28 accessible summits is North Barrule which overlooks the flat plain of Ayre; the most southerly, and westerly, is Cronk ny Arrey Laa where the cliffs drop steeply into the sea. The hills form the ridge, or spine of the Island, that runs on a north east to south west axis. The distance between these two extreme points is only 17 miles as the crow flies which demonstrates the extensive offering for hill walkers contained in such a small area.

The hills offer something for every different circumstance. Many of them can be completed there and back from where you can park your car within an hour or so – say at the end of your working day in the spring and summer. Others can be combined into groups suitable for a half day or a full day of walking. Some ascents are gentle strolls and are ideal for walkers of all ages and abilities, while others offer a little more of a challenge. However, ascending several summits in the same session is no strenuous marathon nor is it a test of stamina.

Despite the Island's small size the weather can vary considerably depending on where you are. So, on a certain day, if it is cloudy over the more southerly hills, North Barrule and Clagh Ouyr in the north could be in bright sunshine and are beckoning you to walk there.

While writing this journal I came across several collective nouns for mountains and hills in the British Isles. Probably the most well-known is 'Munro' designating a Scottish mountain over 3,000 feet which was originally compiled in 1891 by Sir Hugh Munro. But there are many others including 'Marilyns', 'Grahams', Corbetts', 'Deweys' and 'Birketts'.

So let me introduce you to another terms the *'Coopers'*. Numbering 28 the *'Coopers'* are an entirely non- arduous challenge compared with the Munro's of which there are 284. This is a journal of how I climbed the *'Coopers'* over seven part or full days in the late winter and spring of 2014.

My journal of walking the summits

The table lists the summits in descending order of height and indicates a convenient start-point where I parked my car safely. I have also endeavoured to provide a translation of the Manx name – but feel free to use your own interpretation – particularly for Slieau Maggle.

This journal reflects how I combined several hills in the same trip, or did the occasional summit on its own. However, there are other ways to group the peaks to make up a longer walk and so other places where you might want to start your day. I have shown the times that I set off and completed a climb to give an indication of how many hilltops can be achieved in the time that you have available. Don't worry – I was walking at a modest pace, stopping often to make notes and take pictures – so these times are easily achievable.

The maps provide a general overview of that session's walking. The intention is to illustrate the relative positions of the summits and the general direction of the route that I took to ascend and descend. They do not profess to include all observable detail as, in most instances, one's approach to and away from the summits will be apparent as one walks. However, do take the Ordnance Survey map as your security blanket. It will not always be required to chart your route, but it will prove invaluable when it is. Furthermore, the map will help you name all the other hills that you can observe from each hilltop that you have walked to.

I have included photographs primarily as anecdotes about my walk - as practical aids to help fellow walkers navigate to the summits. They are not intended to be of the highest artistic merit – I will leave that challenge for you. The uplands deserve better treatment in photography than I can ever give them.

I wore a light pair of walking boots. Their firm soles and ankle support helped to smooth any rough stretches that I encountered - which weren't many. I selected walking days when the weather forecast was optimistic so my water resistant jacket was only called upon to protect me from the wind or cooler temperatures on the tops. On several days I had no need of it due to the warm weather. There are no refreshment points to be found during the walks so bring with you whatever food and drink that you need to sustain you.

When I walk I always respect the countryside. There is public access to the summits but it is prudent to stick to existing tracks as often as possible to avoid erosion of the land. With only a couple of exceptions, the summits attract very little foot traffic. Fortunately, there are few signs of walking leading to degradation of the terrain. However, paths to a few summits use green lanes or Greenways which permit access for off-road motorbikes and 4 wheel drive vehicles. Here the land can become badly rutted.

The hills of the Island are, unfortunately, the scene of several military plane crashes over the last 70 years – in part due to Manannan's Cloak of fog and low-lying cloud which regularly makes the uplands difficult to see or obscures them completely. There are records of nine aircraft crashes on the northern hills and four on southern summits. As you climb these hills spare a thought for 'Manannan's prisoners'

As the premise of the *'Coopers'* is the imperial unit of feet, I will continue to use this measurement approach in this journal.

THE WALKS

DAY I – 27th February

Cloudy with bursts of sunlight, no rain, but strong gusting wind on the hill tops. I had planned to take a couple of days off work and I was adequately rewarded with good weather for the time of year. The logical place to begin my adventure is at the top – Snaefell leads my catalogue by just under 200 feet over North Barrule.

The Mountain Road (A18) linking Douglas and Ramsey has many good parking spots along its length – largely due to it being the most spectacular stretch of the 37.73 mile TT Course. One of the biggest of these is the car park at what used to be motorcycle museum at a high part of the course referred to as The Bungalow, which happens to be at the foot of Snaefell.

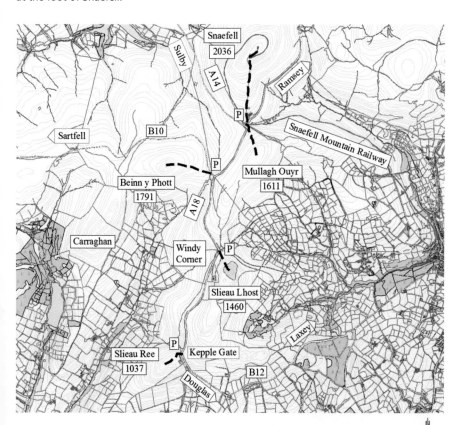

0.85   0.425   0   0.85   1.7   2.55
Miles

Snaefell

I begin my task by tackling the Island's highest summit which is classified as a mountain as it is over 2,000 feet (just). However, it is an easy climb which becomes only moderately steep for last few hundred yards. It makes me ponder why there is such a significant distinction between 'mountain' and 'hill'. The former are invariably referred to in grandiose terms *'I'm setting off to climb a mountain'* whereas hill is a much milder reference *'let's just walk up that hill'*. Despite its official taxonomy Snaefell is really a hill – there is no need to view this ascent as a mountain climb.

This winter has been one of the wettest on record and it rained last night so it is a tad saturated under foot. But as Snaefell is somewhat a national treasure, the path is well maintained so the under foot conditions never slow my progress. The sun is strong (a glorious treat in February) as I climb, with generally high cloud apart from a few wisps clinging to the top of the mountain. If any place on the Island is capped in cloud it is likely to be Snaefell as it is a few hundred feet more elevated than anywhere else.

There is a well-defined track through grass, heather and peat cuttings which starts from a clearly signed kissing gate (P1). Mid-way there is a short passage of slate paving which was glistening with rain and occasionally slippery. I caught sight of a rabbit and a mountain hare, the latter was still all white. There are beautiful views down the

1. The start of my venture

valley, which has been carved by glaciers, towards Laxey, and the old mine workings, and (out of sight) the Isabella Wheel. For the last few hundred feet the path becomes less defined – I prefer to take the track on the right heading towards the left of the two radio masts. On reaching the flat top I walk past the Summit Hotel, which was boarded up for winter, and follow the concrete path and handrail to achieve the trig point. There is a plaque indicating which directions to look to see the adjacent countries. In fact, there is a saying that from Snaefell, on a clear day, one can see the Seven Kingdoms: Mann, Scotland, Ireland, Wales, England, Neptune and Heaven.

As regards the Island itself, a great many of its peaks are visible stretching from North Barrule to its southerly namesake. Indeed, as the hills are so compactly laid out, most of the other individual summits on my travels will afford views of at least a dozen neighbouring hills.

Snaefell is the windiest place on the Island. Gusts in excess of 140 mph were recorded in the winter of 2013/14. When I have climbed Snaefell in previous winters I have seen how the wind had pushed the snow and ice against the side of buildings and fences to create intriguing snow sculptures.

From afar Snaefell is easily recognisable by its pair of radio masts. These form part of the UK Air Traffic Control tracking system and are the first beacons whose radio transmissions are picked up by planes after they have crossed the Atlantic. It is a pity that they are placed on such an elevated and scenic spot, but in the Victorian era the construction of the hotel and the mountain railway set the precedent of having man-made edifices on Snaefell. I suppose that by collecting all these structures in one place all the other summits can continue to remain unspoilt. Another inadvertent benefit of these masts is that, as I conquer the '*Coopers*', they often act like two fingers pointing down from the sky to Snaefell to help me orientate myself and allow me to identify all the other hills in the panorama.

2. Joey Dunlop – King of the Mountain

Alas, this mountain is the site of several plane crashes. An RAF Handley Page Hampden crashed on Snaefell on New Year's Day 1940 killing three crew members and badly injuring the fourth. While an RAF Squadron was re-locating from Duxford in Cambridgeshire to their new base in Northern Ireland on 8th October 1941 two aircraft came to grief here killing four crewmen and on the same day a Wellington flying to its new base from the factory crashed killing its one crewman. On 8th June 1944 a US B24 bomber crashed into Snaefell while re-locating from Lancashire to Northern Ireland and all four crew died.

The descent is by the same route as ascent. To start this I head to final post of the electric railway and proceed left downhill, in my case following an insulated cable on the ground. I soon pick up a proper path. Near the end of my descent I bear left for 50 yards to look at the Joey Dunlop Memorial (P2). Joey, from Ballymoney in Northern Ireland, was arguably the greatest motorbike road racer of all times, he won 26 TT Races a feat which may never be unsurpassed – although John McGuinness is currently closing in on this record. Tragically, he died while riding at a relatively minor road race in Estonia on 2nd July 2000. His funeral was attended by 50,000 mourners. King of the Mountain.

Mullagh Ouyr

I leave the car where it is parked and cross over the Mountain Road to start this easy and brief ascent.

I find the path by walking through the white double gates of railway track. I have no need to look out for trains as the Mountain Railway from Laxey to Snaefell doesn't start running until Easter. I pass through the snicket gate and head towards a gap in a small fence. As these first 50 yards can be quite boggy there is the temptation to take the raised wooden platform, but this only leads to the bridge that crosses the Mountain Road. The way is across grass and heather and I soon reach the top which is marked by a low cairn. For such little effort I am rewarded by sweeping views looking back to Snaefell and the chain of hills culminating in North Barrule.

I return to the car by the same route as I ascended.

Beinn y Phott

Park the car in a lay-by a few yards down the B10 from its junction with the Mountain Road – very close to the Marshal's hut at Brandywell.

Beinn y Phott is my favourite summit for a number of reasons. It is an ascent of barely 15 minutes which means, including the drive from my home in Douglas, the entire trip can be completed in an hour – say in a lunch-break. The going is easy over grassland so it can be walked even after recent rain without getting wet feet. It is not far off the same height as the highest peak Snaefell so it affords very similar views. Yet it is not cluttered by tram rails, radio masts, concrete paths and buildings. Nor by people.

The summit is visible from the car parking spot. I cross the road and walk round to the right of the wooden railing that is there to prevent motorbike access. For the first 50 yards I head slightly to the left of the exact direction of the peak in order to pick up the trail. I stick to this commonly used path all the way to the top. All I encounter are hardy sheep grazing in the distance. Half way along on the left there is a large white boulder on its own which must have been left by the retreating glaciers at the end of the last Ice Age. If I'm out to challenge myself I will complete the ascent in one go without pausing to draw breath and turn to admire the view behind me. Today is one of those days.

The summit is marked by a low cairn with a small collection of rocks which looks like it once acted as a sheep shelter. From here I can see a dozen or so of the 1,000 feet summits in the north and middle of the Island (P3) as well as views of Douglas to the east. The only minor drawback with Beinn y Phott is that the layout of the surrounding hills is particularly efficient at funnelling the sound of the motorbikes as they

3. Beinn y Phott summit and view to Snaefell and North Barrule

enjoy the unrestricted speeds of the Mountain Road several hundred feet below. But on a February morning there are no such intrusions.

A few feet south east of the cairn hides a small rainwater tarn. It is one of the few patches of standing water in the uplands of the Island.

I descend by exactly the same route as I came – heading towards my parked car which is just a smudge in the distance.

Slieau Lhost   11.55 – 12.10

There is a pulling in place on the Mountain Road at Windy Corner by the Marshal's hut (P4).

Windy Corner is aptly named as winds rush up the Baldwin valley over the brow of the hill and down towards Laxey. Although it is a gentle curve on the TT Course, the gusty winds can make it very hazardous for motorbike riders.

I proceed through the gate to right of cattle grid then towards the stone wall into which slate steps have been fixed. I pick my route carefully as the first 50 yards are quite boggy. The path over grass and heather is clearly visible snaking up the hill. A large cairn marks the top, with a walled enclosure built into it to give shelter to any sheep that are brave enough to venture up here. This summit affords the best views of rolling pastureland of Glen Roy in the direction of Laxey and the plantations around the Creg ny Baa Back Road. Not on this day, but often I have been able to see the Lake District hills over to the east across the Irish Sea.

The route down is the same as the route up.

4 Slieau Lhost from the Windy Corner Marshal's hut

Slieau Ree   12.20 – 12.35

I park in a large tarmac'd lay-by next to the Marshal's hut at Keppel Gate as the Mountain Road descends towards Douglas. There is a yellow gate over to the right with a cinder track that leads in the direction of the hill. It is a flat, featureless plateau, so I take a compass reading in order to give the best indication of where to head to achieve the highest point. I walk across heather, some growing quite high, which is intersected by a small stream cutting through the peat.

5. The original Keppel Gate

I judge the summit by eye as there is no cairn to signify the hilltop. Indeed, the spot marked on the OS map with altitude of 316 metres is below the highest point - is it a cartographer's whimsy? I walk to an almost imperceptible edge and am rewarded with a commanding view of Douglas and it's Bay.

In the very early days of the TT Races there was actually a gate here which had to be opened so that racers could continue round the course – hence this section is referred to as Keppel Gate. All that remains now is the gatepost (P5). Apart from the historic significance of the location, I would only recommend spending time here if you are on a mission to bag all the 'Coopers'.

DAY 2 – 28th February

Mainly sunny, occasionally clouding over, dry, hardly any wind. As the forecast was favourable for the whole day I decided to tackle three summits to the south, and four to the north, of Sartfell plantation as one walk. I wonder how many people have looked around the seven hills and suggested that the summits should be linked in a single expedition on foot? The complete circuit of these hills is a wonderful day's walking.

Sartfell is a shy and unpretentious area. It is more remote from a main road than other summit areas. Neither does it seek undue publicity through the fame of its hills. It is somewhat a concealed paradise. However, it has thrown itself open to modern progress as you will discover near Slieau Curn and Slieau Dhoo.

You can approach these summits via the Mountain Road (A18) then take left turn onto B10 at Brandywell. My favourite route is to follow the Baldwin Valley from Strang/Mount Rule on B22. This allows one to

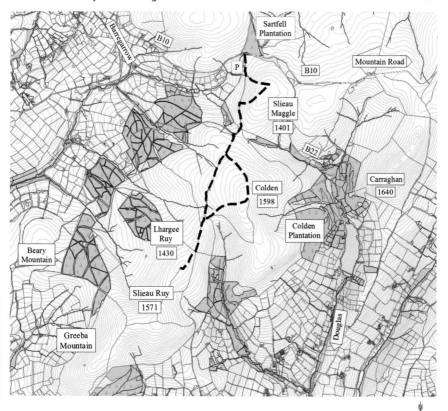

take in the beauty of woodlands and plantations, the West Baldwin reservoir, the river Glass and a gentle waterfall as the road climbs. The River Dhoo joins with the Glass in the east of the Island to give the capital its name. Higher up the road crosses open moorland with views towards Scotland as the junction with B10 is approached. Turn left and in 100 yards on the left there is a gated track where you can park off the road safely.

Also at the junction with the B10 is a narrow unfenced road traveling through Druidale ending at the village of Ballaugh. From my point of view this is the most idyllic road on the entire Island.

Slieau Maggle   10.40 – 11.00

I start the day by walking the southerly hills in this area. I pass through the gate and down the track for approx. half a mile. I find a substantial slate slab on the left that enables me to cross the gully that follows the track (P6). This slab is flanked by two old gate-posts: ignore a smaller slab a couple of hundred yards previously. From here there is a more or less cleared path up a small valley heading east towards the summit. The going is moderately steep, but the valley is dry even in the wet weather that we have been having recently. As I head uphill views of the forestry plantations to the west, the coastland by Kirk Michael and over the Irish Sea open up. I bear slightly to the right as I ascend. The climb levels off as I reach a false summit but the real top can now be spotted a few hundred yards away. The low cairn of white stones has a small pole inserted in its midst. I have breath-taking views of many hills including Snaefell which this morning has a light dusting of snow.

6. Granite slab that marks the way to Slieau Maggle

To proceed to the next summit you could retrace your steps down hill to re-join the track where you left it. I take an alternative route, taking a south west compass bearing to head across the open heather, albeit losing quite a bit of height, towards Colden.

Colden   11.10 – 11.40

As I leave the plateau of Slieau Maggle I soon see the forestry track that I will eventually re-join. On reaching this track I take the right fork towards a gate (marked with a green sign) with a stile to the right. Although tempting, I eschew the footpath to the left indicated by the signpost. After 200 yards there is a gate on the left with a footpath sign. Through the gate and my way is indicated by a post on the horizon.

The initial ascent is easy although the track is a little rutted. After five minutes I see a pile of white stones on the left and an old concrete way marker (ignore the first one). I leave the track here and head left towards the summit. Expanses of cleared heather make this relatively easy walking and, again, there is a false summit. The true peak, which is marked by a low cairn and old telegraph pole, is only 15 minutes further. Again, there are beautiful views of many of the hills that I have climbed yesterday which make up the spine of the Island. To the east are Onchan, Douglas and Douglas Bay.

The hilltops in this area are often marked by telegraph poles as well as cairns. Although cairns can be made relatively easily by transporting individual stones to the summit and gradually forming the landmark, it must have involved a considerable effort to lug a telegraph pole to each summit.

I take a south west compass bearing and make my way cross-country to the next summit. The way towards the summit is marked by posts. I pick my way across the springy heather and tussocky grass towards the forestry track which I re-join to take me onwards to the third summit. The occasional pole acts as a confirmation that I am on the right course.

Lhargee Ruy   11.55 – 12.10

Lhargee Ruy is somewhat special to my family and I – although anonymously so until recently. As we drive or walk home from the centre of Douglas we come down the side street of Selborne Drive. Just before it slopes down to intersect with Quarterbridge Road you have such wonderful views of farm fields, woodland and a hill several miles away. This is a very uplifting sight of countryside from the town. A couple of summers ago I made the effort to locate and climb this hill. And although the panorama from Lhargee Ruy is grand it is not, for me at least, as inspiring as the view of Lhargee Ruy from Selborne Drive.

I am back on the main trail again. The way to Lhargee Ruy can be seen clearly. The ascent to the summit is a grassy track easily seen on the left, with the cairn being readily visible. Along the route there is an old footpath sign post with two bent fingers – it seems a bit odd to see this in the middle of this open moorland but it does confirm that I am on a public right of way. The top marked by a slate cairn with a few white rocks adorning it. From here you can see a cairn a few hundred metres further south but, alas, this does not mark another of the designated summits.

At this point there is the possibility of continuing south to Slieau Ruy and Greeba Mountain. However, this would take me quite a distance from where I left the car. These two hills are accessible from Crosby which will entail far less walking. I decide to leave Lhargee Ruy and go back to re-join the trail and, turning right, I stroll back to where I had left the car to have lunch. Posts indicate the direction of the path, and as my route this morning has been cross-country from summit to summit, this return track is new territory for me.

Sartfell 13.25 – 14.25

I cross over the road (B10) and walk 200 yards left to a gated track on the right. This marks the start of a Green Lane. In this case it is categorised as a Greenway Road. The difference being that vehicle access on a Greenway is restricted, usually from November to March, whereas motorbike and 4 X 4 access in unrestricted on Green Lanes. Walkers, horse riders and mountain bikers can use Greenways at all times. This particular Greenway leads all the way to Ballaugh and on past occasions I have made this the start of a circular walk in its own right.

On reaching Ballaugh on the Greenway, turn right on the main road (A3) and after a short walk take a right turn at the Raven pub to follow a minor road uphill. After a mile the road reaches Ballaugh Plantation where one takes a well-made path that climbs through the forest. On leaving the forest the path takes one towards a minor road (Druidale). Turn right, after 400 yards there is a Green Lane on the right which takes you past Slieau Dhoo and eventually to the road where you parked your car. The walk is approx. 12 miles and is generally easy going, although the ascent through the Ballaugh Plantation is steep in places. It is a very well signed walk.

Today I pursue the track uphill until I reach the end of the plantation. At this point there is a small solar panel attached to a pole. There is no indication what this solar panel powers, it's just there facing south attracting sunshine. I will give a small reward to anyone who can lighten my darkness about its purpose. My meteorological guess is that it is measuring the amount of sunshine that falls on these hills – which is a fair bit today. A few yards past this panel the Greenway bears sharp right - here I leave the track (just before the wooden rail on the left) and head left across the heather towards Sartfell summit.

I catch my first sight of a paraglider floating in the sky several hundred feet above the hills. He moves effortlessly across the sky gaining height then gliding across to another part of the countryside. It is perhaps 8 Celsius here on land, and as he is considerably higher and picking up the winds he might be feeling the chill. I hope that he is not only using, but wearing, thermals to enjoy his flight!

I follow sheep run tracks always heading towards an area of exposed white rocks. After a few minutes later I startle a mountain hare, or more correctly it startles me. It leaps up from his hiding spot only a few yards from where I am. Still largely white, with brown appearing on the tips of his ears, he swiftly bounds 50 yards and stops to survey me. Sensing that I am slow moving and pose no threat he slowly lollops off away from view. I was climbing Sartfell several months later and at almost exactly the same point a hare broke from cover and ran off into the distance. The hare was a mottled brown and

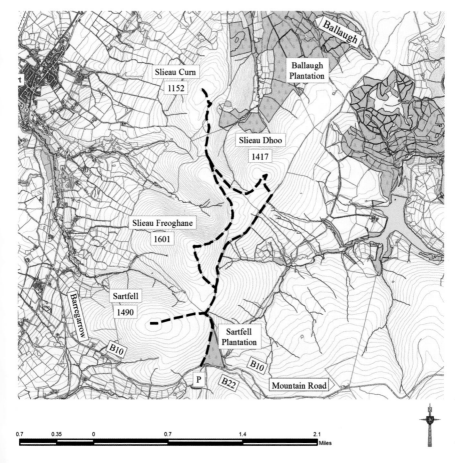

7. You could climb this telegraph pole to have an even higher view at Sartfell

grey colour. (I wonder if it was the same animal after it had changed its white winter coat). As the climb flattens to a plateau the landscape becomes rocky – reminding me of pictures of the lunar landscape taken on the Apollo missions. I now see the characteristic telegraph pole that marks summits in this part of the Island. The iron steps are still in place on the pole so the intrepid walker could actually climb a few yards above the summit if they so wish (P7).

From here there I have a 270 degree panorama of the hills of the north, west and south of the Island – I do have the feeling of being right in the centre of the hilly backbone of the Island. Just to the left of the summit is a small square fenced off area of barren rocky round with no distinguishing features. Again, my eternal gratitude to the first person who can explain the purpose of this enclosed plot. As the top is flat and featureless it is wise to take a compass bearing (ENE) from the summit when heading back to the track for the next hill, Slieau Freoaghane.

Slieau Freoaghane   14.25 - 15.25

Downslope from Sartfell I head towards the small clump of trees that is in front of me and in the general direction of the twin masts atop Snaefell. Towards the bottom of the slope I head towards the wooden fence posts. I reach the Greenway and follow it for half a mile. Initially it gently ascends, then as it levels off there is a small pile of slate rocks by the side on the right: here I bear off the Greenway and pick my own path across the heather towards the high ground of Slieau Freoaghane.

The path steepens as it reaches the shoulder of Slieau Freoaghane. After another 5 minutes I reach the clavicle where the path flattens off and the summit is visible. The final 200 yards is guided by the now familiar telegraph pole. Uniquely this summit boasts the 'holy trinity' of a trig point, cairn and telegraph pole (P8)! The more northerly peaks in this walk afford good views of the flat plains surrounding Ayre, Bride, Andreas and Jurby. Beyond that I can see the white car ferries that cross between Stranraer and Larne – occasionally 2 or 3 are in view. Even in days of moderate visibility one can see the coastline of southern Scotland.

I head east off the summit with the twin radio towers of Snaefell to the left of centre as my way-marker. In front is Sulby Reservoir. This is

the largest reservoir or lake on the Island and is located near the source of the Sulby River, which is the longest river on the island. A clear path leads one back to the Greenway which I join where a wooden rail has been installed to deter vehicles from diverting off the Greenway.

8. A trio of pole, cairn and trig point mark the summit of Slieau Freoaghane

Slieau Curn   15.25 – 15.55

The trail affords quick progress for the one and a quarter miles to the foot of the third hill in this group – Slieau Curn. There is a flat-topped hill on the left just before Slieau Curn. It is not named on the OS map – although some refer to it as Slieau Vael (translated as Michael's Peak) – but is given a spot height (331) so it might be a candidate for inclusion as a *'Cooper'*. Nevertheless, it is a pleasant detour to the top which is marked by a small pile of white stones. There are great views to the south of the sea cliffs near Port Erin.

I can now see four paragliders floating over the hills. To the left I see Kirk Michael on the west coast. This village has a very narrow main street running through it which makes it challenging for both riders and residents during TT Races. I notice dozens of flooded fields that should have cattle or sheep on them but are unoccupied. To the right are the steep, wooded slopes leading down into the Sulby Valley. At the crossing of two Greenways, where there is a wooden gate and a red cattle grid, I carry straight on slightly to the right following the marker posts. This section is marked as 'Road Closed' during autumn and winter – closed to motor traffic to allow the deeply rutted path to repair itself – but walkers can continue

First the track descends then it ascends. It passes through two metal gateposts and after a concentrated grouping of wooden posts I

17

bear left off the track towards Slieau Curn. There is no obvious path so I use a tract of cleared heather in the direction of the higher ground. After no more than 5 minutes I spot the reassuring sight of a telegraph pole – albeit highly weathered. The way up is across low heather and the summit is soon reached: it sports a modest cairn and pole. I leave the high point and head east with the twin towers of Snaefell, as a sighter, just to my left to regain the Greenway.

Slieau Dhoo   15.55 – 16.25

On regaining the track I turn tight heading towards the final hill top. I reach the crossroad that I passed less than 20 minutes ago and take the left fork, again marked 'Road Closed' in certain seasons. This grass track is deeply rutted so much so that motor vehicles have carved tracks 15 yards wide making it quite a challenge for the walker to find flat terrain. I ponder if there will ever be an amicable way in which walkers and bikers can share the same paths in the countryside. Or indeed if motorbike riders should be allowed off-road access at all in grassland areas like this.

On the Island there is a Green Lane User Group (GLUG) which believes that *"all users of the countryside can enjoy their pastime without upsetting others, and without destroying the green lanes themselves"*. Unfortunately, this stretch of countryside is evidence of vehicle users enjoying their pastime while upsetting walkers. The Manx Government is unlikely to step in to impose stronger restrictions on off-road motorbike as motorsport is so much part of the Island's heritage and DNA.

As I negotiate this section on my left, partially in shade as the sun is only low in the sky, there is a precipitously sloped valley with the thin ribbon of a stream in the bottom – mountain sheep territory only. On reaching the head of this valley (where there is a fence and a wooden gate on my right) I bear left to make my own ascent up the slope of Slieau Dhoo. I head north picking my own path across the heather and tussocks of grass. After a moderately stiff climb for the last few yards I achieve the small flat summit. Here there is a small rainwater tarn (P9). If I had had the foresight to bring a towel I might have taken my boots off and had a paddle – but only a briefly as the water is definitely very cold. Adjacent to the cairn is a 10 foot deep depression which must be natural but, unlike the adjacent tarn, it does not hold any water. It is probably used by sheep taking shelter from the winter winds.

I meet a couple on the summit who are looking for frog spawn in the boggy wetland – it takes all sorts to make a world.

I head south east from the top to regain the Greenway track and

9. Rainwater tarn on Slieau Dhoo

turn right and walk in the direction of the setting sun. I encounter an altogether bolder mountain hare who is sunning himself on the track but dashes off (or should I say hares off) when I approach. I follow this track all the way back to the car without encountering a soul or hearing a sound. All the while with wonderful views of the near uninhabited Druidale to my left. Return to car **17.25.**

DAY 3 – 2nd March
Slieau Whallian   11.00 – 12.15

This walk is best tackled after a dry spell as the tracks through the plantation can become very muddy.

   A cloudy day which obscures the tops of the hills to the north and south but Slieau Whallian escapes 'Manannan's Cloak'. As it is to the west and a slightly lower elevation than other summits it is the only one that offers itself up to me today.

   The lower part of the route to the top takes one through Slieau Whallian Plantation. I enjoy woodland walking as a contrast to the open moorlands which characterise the other summits. This forest dominates the skyline when you are standing on Tynwald Green in St John's. Tynwald is our Parliament and it is alleged that that it was originally held here in the open air in 979. Parliament now conducts its business indoors in a purpose built building in Douglas, known locally as the 'wedding cake'. However, on the Manx National Day an open air ceremony is held on Tynwald Green at which any resident can address the Parliament which assembles there to request that a new law is considered.

Two ways through this forest are described. Both of them culminate in steep tugs to the edge of the plantation – definitely for the more determined walker.

The obvious route is to start on the main forest track. This is found by taking the A30 towards Patrick and immediately after a hump back bridge take the minor road on the left: a little way up this road on the right a sign shows the plantation's name. This is a well-used access which winds its way uphill through the forest. Ignore the wide grassy tracks off to the left and right and keep climbing. As the track levels off and begins to bear right take an unmarked but well-worn path on the left that cuts through the trees. This heads towards a moss covered dry stone wall. Carry on uphill with the wall on your right, ignoring any flatter routes to your left and right. For the last several hundred yards you have to pick your own way over this steep hill, trying your best to

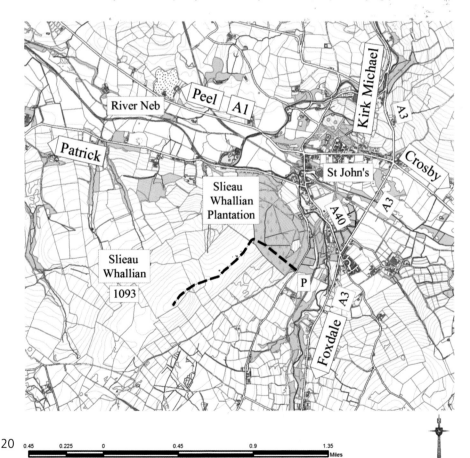

0.45   0.225   0   0.45   0.9   1.35
                                          Miles

avoid fallen trees, heading towards the light which signifies the end of the canopy of trees.

The ascent that I take today entails driving further up the minor road until the end of the plantation: 200 yards further on there is a pull in area by Slieau Whallian Farm. I walk back down the road a little and at the edge of the plantation there is a gate on the left leading onto a Greenway path. After 200 yards there is a gap in the gorse hedge on the right and a fence and low wall about 40 yards away. On reaching the wall I cross the stile which takes me into the woods. I bear slightly left so that the dry stone wall that bounds the plantation is visible. I now pick my way uphill keeping the wall about 20 yards away on my left. As I climb through the forest I hear that eerily wonderful sound of wind rushing through the trees. But as the trees are so tightly grouped there is hardly a breath of wind in the forest itself. Several dry stone walls meander across the woodland; they are now almost entirely covered in green moss (P10). Towards the last stages of the woodland climb I keep closer to the wall and on reaching the perimeter fence at the top bear right for a couple of hundred yards to find the stile that takes me onto the open land leading to Slieau Whallian summit.

A sign confirms that walkers are allowed on the summit by the landowners although there is no right of way. I take a brief detour to the right to admire an enormous and carefully built cairn (P11). There is no obvious reason for a cairn to be here. However, legend has it that this is the site where if a woman was suspected of being a witch she was placed in a spiked barrel and rolled down the hill. If she died she was regarded as being innocent, but if she survived she would be declared a witch and would have been burnt at the stake.

Heading up hill I see a post indicating that there is a stile to take me over the dry stone wall. The summit is reached by a path picking its way through the heather. A flat top to the hill and large cairn marks

my destination. I look down on Peel and its harbour and across to the coast of Ireland.

I retrace my steps from the top, eschewing the temptingly wider track which does not take you back to where you started. I re-enter the plantation and pick my own way over fallen trees to join the main track downhill. It is easier to follow this broad track down to the main entrance of the plantation rather than retrace the meandering ascent that I took earlier to make my ascent. On leaving the plantation I turn right on the minor road and walk back to the car.

DAY 4 – 17th April

Bright and dry day with high cloud, occasional rays of sunshine cut through, fairly windy. Again, my planned day off work is rewarded with good weather. Today I am tackling peaks in three different areas with contrasting walking terrains.

For the first hills I park the car just off the A23 near its junction with a minor road heading towards Glen Vine.

Slieau Ruy and Greeba Mountain   9.15 – 11.25

Had I had the necessary stamina and time I might have climbed these hills as part of my sojourn in Sartfell on Day 2. But as I do not regard walking the hills of the Island as a physical challenge, rather a pleasure to be extended as long as possible, I have 'saved them up' for another day.

My walk begins by following a track signed as 'unsuitable for motor vehicles'. In practice this tarmac'd road could be, and is, driven along although it is only the width of one car. The road undulates for a mile and a half and passes a farm on the right at which point the ascent becomes noticeably steeper. I meet the first of four gates where the way becomes a path for walkers and horses but not, we are told by a sign on the gate, for motorbikes. This bodes well for the rest of the walk.

The panorama opens up with sheep grazing on the fields downslope and the hills of the centre of the Island in front of me. After the fourth gate the path is bounded by a dry stone wall on the right. After five minutes I pass an old style concrete yellow way-marker on my right and the path curves gently to the left. Here the wall has fallen down for 10 yards or so: on the left I have made a small pile of white stones to mark the beginning of a narrow track that leads through the heather on the way to Slieau Ruy (P12). After a few yards this widens to a broad grassy swathe that stretches uphill. It is a moderately steep climb through the heather – if in doubt about which way to head favour the right as I did. After ten minutes the ascent flattens and I see the Ordnance Survey column and a large cairn marking the summit. This is actually one of two hills over 1,000 feet high named Slieau Ruy, the other being in the northern part of the Island. Behind me are some of the best views of

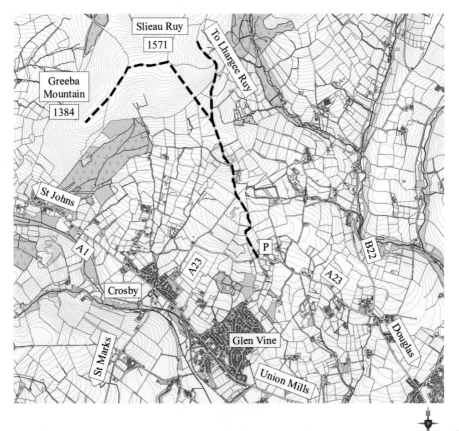

12. The white stones on the left of the track indicate where to strike uphill for Slieau Ruy

the east of the Island including Douglas Bay and the flatter land to the south where the ancient capital of Mann, Castletown, is located.

Unfortunately, this area is also the site of the crash of an Avro Anson based at Jurby on 3rd January 1946: two crewmen and two passengers were killed.

I take a compass bearing of south west off the summit to make my way to Greeba Mountain which is clearly visible. This is only a self-styled mountain as it is well short of the 2,000 feet required to be officially designated so. Initially, I follow a wide track which heads slightly west of the next summit but soon I take a narrower track on the left. From this vantage point I can see both the east coastline where Douglas and

13. South Barrule and Cronk ny Arrey Laa viewed from Greeba Mountain

24

Onchan sit and the west where Peel lies. The summit is reached by a very gentle ascent and is marked by a low cairn. I can see the most southerly summits of South Barrule and Cronk ny Arrey Laa (P13).

I retrace my route back to Slieau Ruy and thence down across the heather to regain the path that follows the dry stone wall. As I leave the grassy path a sign on the gate shouts 'Caution Hazard' – presumably to alert you that you are re-joining a road on which you might encounter a car!

In just over two hours I have not encountered another soul although I am no more than a five minute drive from the capital, Douglas.

Slieau Managh and 336   13.15 – 15.15

Cloudy, windy but dry to start with, begins to drizzle on the latter part of the walk. There is off-road parking by the Mountain Box Marshal's hut on the Mountain Road (A18).

The ascent starts by following a green lane with a kissing gate on the right of the main gate. I follow the track across flat open terrain, initially on tarmac then a rocky surface, in places heavily rutted by motorbikes. I keep the dry stone wall on my right and follow the

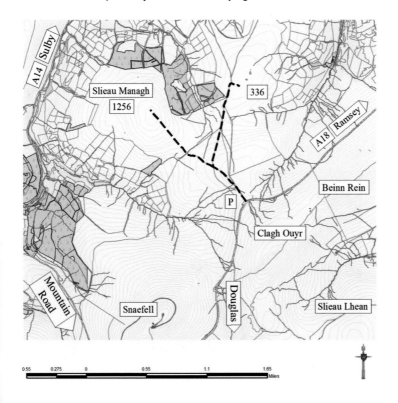

Greenway signs. The track falls down into a shallow dip and bears right to blend into the much wider Millennium Way long distance path. Here I take a well-trodden grassy path on the left, I can just about make out the shape of a cairn on the skyline. Views open up of the Plain of Ayre to the north. This has the feeling of being quite a remote place as the panorama comprises few settlements of any size.

There is soon a slight incline towards the flat hill top. I follow parallel tracks which look as though they were made by horse and cart traffic many decades ago. Grassland gives way to heather. The modest cairn which marks the expansive summit area is now visible.

On retracing my steps the way that I came, I notice a baby's dummy on the path – seemingly anyone can tackle this gentle ascent (P14)!

On re-joining the wider track I turn right on the Millennium Way path towards the summit simply referred to by its height – 336 (metres). 336 is the most optional of the *'Coopers'*. Although there is a spot height marked on the OS map when one reaches the flat open summit there is no visible sign of the highest point.

The rutted path falls downhill then gradually climbs up again. At the lowest point there is a raised wooden walkway that takes one straight ahead over the boggy land. I walk through a metal kissing gate on to the open heather and leave the plantation behind me over my left shoulder. At the second of two nearby signs indicating a public footpath on the left I take a path on my right over the open heather. There is evidence that others have walked this way before me, but those others might be sheep. As there is no cairn or post to indicate a high point you can say 'summit accomplished' at any time. The tumulus marked on the OS map is not visible to my eye, but instead there is a great view of the chain of hills culminating in North Barrule.

14. Seemingly anyone can tackle the gentle ascent of Slieau Managh

I return to the Greenway and turn left to return to the car heading dead in line with Snaefell. I remember to turn left off the Millennium Way to follow the Greenway back to Mountain Box hut.

Beary Mountain   15.50 – 18.50

The weather has brightened up later on in the afternoon, or else it's the difference of having travelled a few miles to the west of the Island. I park off the road in Little London which is a turning off the B10 just before Barregarrow. Little London is in complete contrast to its big brother in England, as it is a collection of a few farm buildings. Was London like this 5,000 years ago?

I take a track over the bridge where there is a footpath sign for Crosby resting at a gentle angle. After a couple of hundred yards I'm confronted by a padlocked gate without a stile. The hill walker's

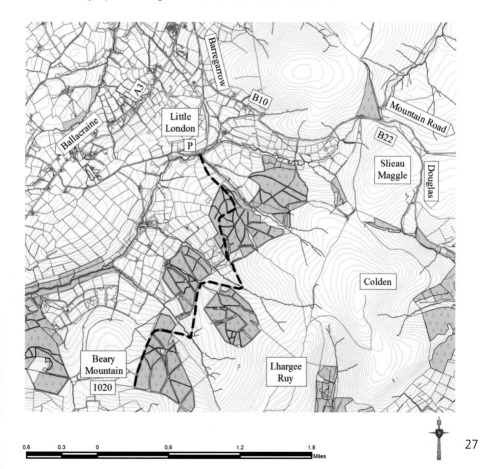

quandary is quickly resolved by a farm worker who confirms that this is a public right of way. I clamber over the gate and follow the path upwards passing a genuine public footpath sign, so doubly legitimising my walk. I go through another gate, this time not locked, and over a stile and a mini bridge to reach a path through the plantation.

When the path joins a wider track used by forestry vehicles I bear right. There are Christmas trees of all shapes and sizes lining the route. The track passes through two gates which carry an official notice warning of 'sudden oak death' and the precautions that should be taken. I carry on along the track ignoring other ones leading off to the left. There are superlative views of the countryside to the west, made all the more pleasurable as one has not had to make a steep ascent to enjoy them.

Over a stile and I leave the plantation to walk in open heather land with views up to Greeba Mountain and Slieau Ruy. A wooden footbridge crosses the sparkling Blaber River. I encounter another padlocked gate but this has a stile to the right. The path forks left uphill – don't be tempted by the right fork downhill.

The OS map indicates that I am now in a Forestry Division plantation. Not all plantations grow in such regular shapes as indicated by maps, trees can thrive in certain locations but struggle to colonise land only a few hundred yards away. I am surmising that this has happened here as heather grows where the map suggests woodland. I continue ascending ignoring two tracks to the left. The path reaches a flat summit area: this is Beary Mountain on which the OS map shows a high point of 311 metres – at 1,020 feet this is the lowest 'Cooper' – definitely a Mini Cooper. I can see no cairn or pole that might mark the highest point.

I feel a little deflated as I wander over the flat summit trying, unsuccessfully, to locate a confirmation of my achievement. But the countryside is not like towns or villages. Mercifully, it is not festooned with signs that tell you where you are. So I can't complain when Beary Mountain retains its summit as a secret.

I retrace the path, remembering to bear right onto the track that I used earlier which is conveniently marked by a yellow Manx Gas pipeline sign. Towards the end of my journey I bear left off the forest track at the footpath sign that points to my left and follow this over stile and bridge back to the field where I began my journey.

DAY 5 – 18th April

A warm and sunny Good Friday, only a few clouds. Plenty of parking available at Black Hut on the Mountain Road (A18).

It is advised to walk the four summits of Clagh Ouyr, 550 (locally known as Beinn Rein or Clagh Ouyr North Top), 533 (no local name is recorded on official maps) and North Barrule in one venture. However, a reader has suggested that '553' is known by fell runners as is Cronk y Chorree Farraghytyn (translated as Hill of Everlasting Wrath). They are very close together with only one obvious easy start point – that being the climb up Clagh Ouyr. The walking is generally easy, although close to the summits it becomes moderately steep for a few minutes, so tackling four in one go involves little real effort.

Given the 'fame' of North Barrule and that it is the first public holiday of the year, with good weather to boot, this proves to be by far my most sociable day of walking. I nod and chat to far more people

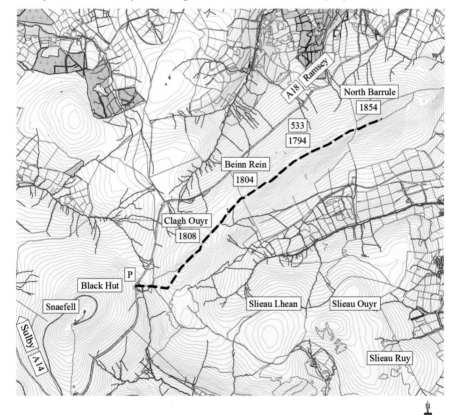

on this one day than all the other six combined. But their companionship is not intrusive – for long periods of time I am alone.

Clagh Ouyr   13.25 – 13.45

I cross the Mountain Road carefully: there is no speed limit so cars and bikes can come upon you very suddenly. There is a stile and a public footpath sign (P15), after 10 yards cross over the dry stone wall at the point where it has fallen so that the wall is now on your right. The first few hundred yards is pretty boggy so I pick my way carefully. Cross over a small wooden walkway cum bridge and take the path bearing left and again in 20 yards bear left to escape the worst of the boggy terrain. Through a gap in the dry stone wall and I am now in open grassland. As the top of Clagh Ouyr is visible it becomes very clear where to head.

A low cairn marks the top of Clagh Ouyr and there is a plaque to remember David 'The Doc' Young left by Manx Fell Runners. As the plaque is not secured to anything I keep on noticing it is in slightly different places each time that I return to the hill.

Alas, Clagh Ouyr has been the scene of two military plane crashes. An Avro Anson plane based at Jurby crashed on a flight from Millom in Cumbria on the 6th September 1953: all four crew members died. A Hawk of No.4 Flying Training School, flew into the hill on the 24th June 1983 killing both crewmen.

It is very simple to navigate to successive summits as each is clearly in view from the previous one. There are expansive views of the north of the Island, the flat plains dotted by villages such as Bride, Andreas and Jurby. Beyond Ramsey is the Point of Ayre lighthouse and beyond that one can see the ferries that cross the Irish Sea between Stranraer and Belfast.

15. The start of the climb to Clagh Ouyr

Beinn Rein (or Clagh Ouyr North Top) and summit '533'
13.45 – 14.25

The route onwards is gently undulating and is marked by small cairns which support larger upright stones. There are no obvious signs, like large cairns or OS trig points that signify that one has reached these two spots marked on the map.

On the right I see the track of the Snaefell Mountain Railway following the side of the valley carved by glaciers which holds the Laxey River. The name Laxey is derived from the Norse word Laxa meaning Salmon River.

The terrain is tussocky grassland which is prone to retaining dampness. After descending Clagh Ouyr I cross particularly wet ground using a raised wooden walkway. I notice a couple of small ponds on the right that look to be a very inviting place to cool my feet in this warm weather. Another stile takes me through a gap in the dry stone wall. I pass one then a second upright slate, supported by a few other prone ones, that signify that I'm heading in the right direction. As the path levels off one can judge that you have reached the flat summit of Beinn Rein.

I pass another upright slate and head downslope past a couple of small stretches of standing water on the left. Two more vertical slates later I guess that I have reached '533'.

North Barrule   14.25 – 14.50

I pass two more slate 'way markers' then over another stile and through a dry stone wall for the final climb to the top of North Barrule. This time the summit is marked by a tall white Ordnance Survey

16. The panorama of Ramsey from North Barrule

column. Unlike many of the relatively flat hilltops on the Island North Barrule is quite precipitous – turning it into an awe-inspiring view as one approaches it.

I have a breath-taking panorama of Ramsey with Queens Pier stretching out into the sea and the sandy red low cliffs to the north (P16). To the east is the flat farmland leading to Maughold and Cornaa and the other hamlets that lie on the coast road from Laxey to Ramsey.

Perhaps at this point I should have recited the Manx National Anthem

> *O land of our birth,*
> *O gem of God's earth,*
> *O Island so strong and so fair;*
> *Built firm as Barrule,*
> *Thy Throne of Home Rule*
> *Makes us free as thy sweet mountain air.*

Alas, I had failed to bring a song sheet with me, so my companions on the summit were spared! I also confess to feeling slightly distanced by the first line of the anthem. Like half the Island's population I was born elsewhere and moved here. Perhaps only Manx born are permitted to sing the anthem, the rest of us are excused from learning it.

I return by the same route, ascending the three summits again. As I am now walking in a completely different direction I enjoy a different set of views to the ones that I had only an hour or so earlier. The re-ascent of Clagh Ouyr is a tad monotonous but doing so does leave you with the achievement of having scaled seven peaks in three hours. One could take a short cut down to the right towards the Mountain Road: however, it is not recommended as the land is boggy in places and not as easy to traverse as it might first look. Return to car **16.25**.

South Barrule   **17.15 – 18.00**

It continues to be a beautiful warm and sunny day, so I decide to drive south to climb North Barrule's sibling.

The Isle of Man has more than its fair share of myths, legends and fairy stories. On one of my walks my contemplations have wandered to likening the twenty eight hills to a group or community of twenty eight giants.

This was probably prompted in my mind by the legend surrounding the formation of Lough Neagh in Northern Ireland which is the largest freshwater lake in the British Isles. As the tale goes Finn McCool, the legendary Irish warrior, after encountering a Scottish giant, scooped up a handful of earth and threw it at his retreating foe. The depression this handful left in the ground was filled by rainwaters and became

Lough Neagh. The earth that had been dug up and thrown at the giant by Finn McCool fell into the Irish Sea to become the Isle of Man. Interestingly, the Isle of Man and Lough Neagh are not too dissimilar in their shapes.

Back to my musings on the Island's twenty eight giants. Two of these were brothers named Barrule. The younger brother called South was incessantly bragging that he was tougher and stronger than his older sibling North. Eventually the community became fed up with these spats so it was decided to resolve it once for all with a bare fist duel. North asked his trusted friend Clagh Ouyr to be his second while South picked Conk ny Arrey Laa to be his. The fight raged long and hard, often with the combatants unable to control their rage and strength and hitting out wildly. On one such occasion, an innocent bystander, the relatively slight Slieau Whallian, was caught accidentally

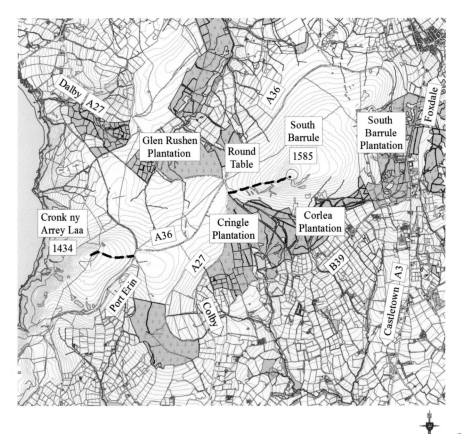

and was hurled into the distance. Eventually, being 250 feet taller, North prevailed and was declared the winner. As punishment for the defeat South and his second were banished far away from the community. Which is why I have reasoned that South Barrule and Cronk ny Arrey Laa are the only major summits (adjacent to each other) in the south of the Island while the remainder are closely gathered in the centre and north. Apart from, that is, Slieau Whallian which has not been able to return from its isolated location in the west where it has been thrown accidentally.

I park the car at the Round Table which is at the junction of the A36 and A27.

The ascent is easy with only a small amount of moderately steep climbing towards the end. There is a wooden gate marked with the name of the hill and its altitude. Beyond this I follow a path through the low heather, at a small ditch I pick up the path slightly to the left of the one that I have been following. When this joins a wider track I bear left. I mark this spot with a couple of stones so that I do not miss it when I return.

Behind are views of an active slate quarry surrounded by Cringle Plantation with a small reservoir adjacent. Beyond this is flat plain holding Castletown, the Langness Peninsula and Ronaldsway Airport. Having come from the hills of the north I am reminded that Jurby and Ronaldsway, which are both surrounded by extensive flat terrain and were used in World War 2, vied with each other to become the Island's civil airport. Ronaldsway was presumably chosen as it was closer to the capital, Douglas: although Jurby's supporters claimed that is would have been a better choice as it is less often cloaked in fog.

In the distance on my left are some ruined buildings and towers signifying the old mines of Foxdale. Here galena and semi-precious crystals were mined in 19th century, whereas in other parts of Foxdale lead and sliver were obtained.

I head towards the crag on the skyline although it is not my end destination. A couple of hundred yards beyond this the summit is marked by a trig point almost completely encircled by a low wall (P17). To the side there is a plaque marking the spot where a Celtic Iron Age Hill Fort was excavated in 1960-61. This is also the unmarked site of the crash of a Vickers Wellington on the 22nd December 1944 during a navigation exercise: all four crew died.

As I descend by the same route and I look straight towards the other summit in the south of the Island Cronk ny Arrey Laa. I remember to turn right off the main track onto the narrower path at the point that that I had previously marked with a few stones.

Cronk ny Arrey Laa   18.15 –18.45

I drive a mile or so further south on the A36 and park the car on an unmarked road just as the main road takes a sharp left turn. This summit is a very gentle ascent.

I walk briefly on the road past the 'Welcome to Rushen' sign and go through a snicket gate on the right to follow the wide clear track straight ahead. It is no time at all before I reach the hilltop. Curiously the Ordnance Survey column does not mark the highest elevation, that task is performed by a large cairn a couple of hundred yards further on. From here I have awesome views of the sea cliff coastline of the south west of the Island extending all the way to the Calf of Man. This is one of the most dramatic views of coastline from any summit, best seen as the sun is sinking in the west – I drink it all in (P18).

18. This photograph struggles to do justice to the view south from Cronk ny Arrey La

Despite its relatively low altitude compared to the peaks in the north, there are records of three aircraft that have crashed into Cronk ny Arrey Laa – I imagine because it is very close to extremely steep sea cliffs. Two crashes were during the WW2: one involved a US Airforce plane killing six crewmen on 4th July 1944; another was an RAF plane on a training exercise on 13th November 1944 in which five died. A civilian cargo plane transporting milk from Northern Ireland to Liverpool crashed on 28th September 1948 killing all 4 crew.

I take the same route to descend, ignoring the footpath sign as it does not lead back to where the journey started. I see Peel to my left and in front as far, as the eye can see, is the chain of hills that form the backbone of the Isle of Man. For such a brief expenditure of time and effort this summit rewards the walker magnificently.

DAY 6 – 20th April

A bright rather than sunny day, cloudy, rain held off until end of trip.

I park in Black Hut car park by the Mountain Road (A18), as I did for the walk to North Barrule and its fellow hilltops. The walking is generally easy. Although there is a clear path leading me around the hills, at appropriate points I will need to use a compass to take a bearing and find my way to the summits.

Slieau Lhean and its colleagues are a little discovered treat. For most people, if they pick this particular spot in the Island for a hill walk it is because they want to experience the quadruple summits that culminate in the august North Barrule. It seems almost perverse to eschew those talents on one's left and instead to bear right towards the less obvious. However, those that do so will be amply rewarded with unique views to the east of the Island – and the most complicated footpath way marker that you will ever encounter.

Slieau Lhean   12.10 – 13.00

I cross the Mountain Road carefully and over the stile marked by the footpath sign. Heading uphill over slightly wet ground I keep the wall on my right apart from the first few yards. I reach the signpost by the wall and this time I take the path to the right – doubtless this is the one less travelled. I head up the hill taking a bearing of 140 degrees just to ensure that I'm on the right course. After a couple of hundred yards the track becomes much more obvious.

There is a splendid panorama of the famous section of the TT Course known as the Verandah, a series of very fast sweeping curves. I notice evidence of motorbike tyre tracks but this is not marked as a green lane on my map. To my right is probably the best view that one can have of the Mountain Railway and at the moment there is a train making its way slowly down the steep slope to the terminus in Laxey.

Further along there is the busiest way marker post that I have ever encountered, it has five pointers marking different footpaths and bridleways (P19)! My track is the one to the right of straight ahead which curiously someone has marked with a traffic cone. The path becomes a rock strewn track along which you could probably drive a 4X4. After 5 minutes there is a pair of posts either side of the track, the remains of an iron gate. I judge that this is as good a place as any to make my own way left across the heather to reach Slieau Lhean summit. There is an old boundary post which I head for in the absence of any other marker on this flat hill top. A couple of hundred yards slightly to the right is a piece of ground minutely more elevated and a wee cairn which I take to be marking the highest point.

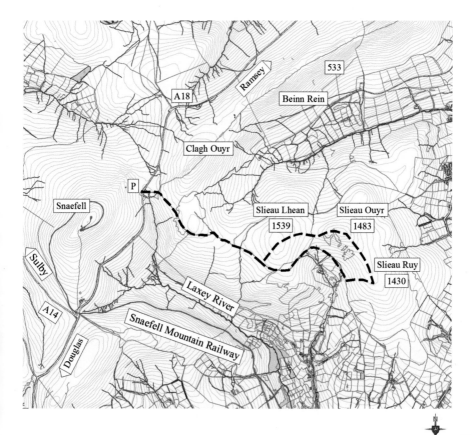

0.7   0.35   0   0.7   1.4   2.1
Miles

Slieau Ouyr   13.00 – 13.20

From there I follow a gently undulating route across the heather
tussocks to the next hill top. I notice the occasional boot print in the
mud which confirms that others have taken this cross-country
approach. On this stretch I encounter a total of four mountain hares
that leap up from their covering of heather and bound away into the
distance. They are still predominantly white which provides absolutely
no camouflage against the dark brown colour of the ground – an
ordinary hare would be practically invisible here. The heather is rarely
more than ankle high and it springs back to its former shape when
walked over, so no harm done. It is also cleans my walking boots very
efficiently.

I pick up a thin grassy track which is heading uphill and makes the
ascent relatively easy. There are a few small cairns on the right to mark
the direction to follow. Opening up in front now are views of Laxey
Bay. The summit cairn is very low but has a protruding slate pointing to
the heavens like a finger. On it someone has chalked a white arrow to
point one in the direction of Slieau Ruy.

Slieau Ruy   13.20 – 13.40

I soon pick up a well-used track heading to the final summit. This is the
second hill named Slieau Ruy that I have climbed, the first was on my
second day adjacent to Greeba Mountain. I would love to know why
two hills carry the same name – perhaps it was to commemorate two
different kings – Translated from Manx Slieau Ruy means King's Hill.

A cairn or two on the path confirms that I am heading in the right

20. View towards Laxey Bay from Slieau Ruy

direction. There is a white covering on the surface of the peat; it is grainy to taste, not salty, unsure what it really is. Beautiful birdsong on this hill, I think that it is a skylark – how I wish that I knew more, or just something, about birds. There is a bit of confusion as to exactly where the summit is. I first pass a humble standing stone, but a couple of hundred yards further there is a large cairn, although that seems to be on slightly lower ground. I travel on to this cairn just to be sure. I am rewarded with the best possible views of Laxey Bay (P20)

I make my way in a westerly direction across the heather towards the wide track which is clearly visible at the side of the valley below me. This part is definitely for those who do not mind improvising their own way, occasionally there are sheep tracks to follow but they soon peter out. The rocky track leads me for several miles towards my journey's start-point. As I reach the Island's most complicated footpath sign the way becomes a grassy path for the final part of the trek back to the car park (return to car **15.30**).

DAY 7 – 25th April

Today I am taking the morning off work to catch up on the one hill that I have omitted up to now. Not because it is an unduly arduous climb nor in a remote part of the Island. No it was simply that my trusty old OS map was so well-used and creased such that the contours and name of this summit had been completely worn away! I only discovered this when, a few days earlier, I had rewarded myself with a new OS map to mark, what I thought at the time was, the conclusion of my adventure. It turned out to be a purchase of great serendipity.

39

Chilly day, some wind, cloud settling at about 1,800 feet means the summit will be fine to climb.

I park safely off the B10 as close as I can to the signpost indicating the Millennium Way footpath, which runs from Ramsey to Castletown a distance of approximately 28 miles. The Manx Millennium was in 1979 a full 21 years ahead of the rest of the world's celebrations of the Millennium! In that year there was the 1,000 year anniversary of parliament on the Isle of Man, which nowadays is commemorated by the annual open-air assembly at Tynwald.

From the road I follow the path over gently undulating grassland. I pass an old-fashioned concrete footpath marker which sheep evidently use as a scratching post. At a three-fingered signpost this path joins a wider gravelly Greenway – there are a series of posts crossed by a

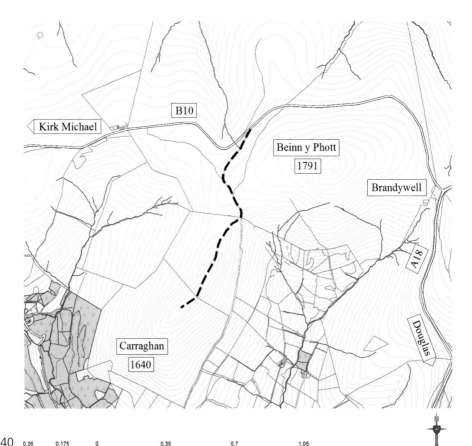

horizontal beam that looks rather like a handrail. I guess that they are here not to steady the walker but to run across the path to stop motorbike riders from deviating off the Greenway and on to the footpaths. Mark this junction in your mind for the return journey.

I head left along the Greenway and go through a wooden gate and bear right along a track that other walkers have used skirting to the right of the 'handrail'. There are sections of handrail across this path, which seem to be doing a good job as the ruts left by motorbikes are beginning to self-repair. It's a flattish summit with a low cairn at the end to mark the point of highest elevation.

The panorama down into the beautiful Baldwin Valley and beyond to Douglas Bay is a copious reward for this short hike. The tranquillity up here is occasionally punctuated by the sound of gunfire from the rifle range across the valley near Windy Corner. I re-trace my steps exactly heeding the signpost and 'handrail' that signify my path off the right of the Greenway.

That's it – the final summit has been reached and my journey is complete. Perhaps this does not afford the most awesome of views that I have encountered on this venture, but very satisfying nevertheless and it is so peaceful up here. I suppose that if I had planned this properly, rather than taken to the hills whenever I had some spare time, I would have ended at North Barrule with its amazing panorama of the north of the Island. Or perhaps Cronk ny Arrey Laa which has a magical view of the cliff coastline of the south west corner of the Island. However, there is satisfaction to be enjoyed in reaching each and every summit and being able to look out across this beautiful Island.

Postscript

Having climbed all the *'Coopers'* – a great many of them several times over – perhaps I am now permitted the self-indulgence of listing my favourites. With only a couple of exceptions all the climbs were entertaining and all hilltops offered wonderful and memorable views, so this is a tough choice. Nevertheless, here is my personal top five, in ascending order.

Lhargee Ruy has given my family and I so much pleasure looking up to it as we drive back home from Douglas. As it was one of my first views of the hills when we moved to the Isle of Man it has probably done more than any other to ignite my interest in hill walking.

Snaefell is the highest point on the Island and, as such, one can look down on all the other summits. And in clear weather it is the only place where one can look across to Scotland, England, Wales and Ireland.

North Barrule is the end of a chain of four hilltops which makes for a very satisfying walk. It also offers sumptuous views of the north of the Island.

Cronk ny Arrey Laa provides such uniquely gorgeous views of the sea cliffs, and does so without requiring you to expend much walking effort. Head there towards the end of a clear day as the sun begins to set and you will struggle to find a better view in the entire British Isles. Of all the hills **Beinn y Phott** is my soul mate – if a hill can be one. A short drive followed by a brief walk and I am in such a beautiful place which affirms to me the enviable quality of life that we have on the Isle of Man.

But which are your favourites?

And now over to you

The greatest reward for climbing all the summits over 1,000 feet will be the awesome views and panoramas, and the lasting memories that they will bring. But second to this, a tangible evidence of your performance is available. If you contact me (details below) I can supply you with signed, dated and numbered Certificate of Achievement. Proof will be a short conversation about your experience.

If you are planning to come over to the Isle of Man to walk the hills I do have Government accredited self-catering and bed and breakfast accommodation where I live in Douglas.

For either of these please contact me on
Email: thealancooper@manx.net
01624 623220